Pearson Primary Progress and Assess

Year 2

Reading

Assessment Guide

Dee Reid and Kate Ruttle

ALWAYS LEARNING   PEARSON

Published by Pearson Education Limited, 80 Strand, London, WC2R 0RL.

www.pearsonschools.co.uk

Text © Pearson Education Limited 2015

Designed by Wild Boar Design Ltd
Original illustrations © Pearson Education Limited 2015
Cover illustration © Pearson Education Limited 2015

First published 2015

18 17 16
10 9 8 7 6 5 4 3 2

British Library Cataloguing in Publication Data

A catalogue record for this book is available from the British Library

ISBN 9780435172930

Printed in the UK by Ashford Colour Press

Acknowledgements
The author and publisher would like to thank the following individuals and organisations for permission to reproduce photographs in the Year 2 reading tests:

(Key: b-bottom; c-centre; l-left; r-right; t-top)

Yr2_OB Shutterstock.com: bojangles, **Art: Dave Pratt. Yr2_WB 123RF.com:** rustyphil, **Art: Dave Pratt. Yr2_PA Alamy Images:** Chronicle, **Art: Dave Pratt. Yr2_PA 123RF.com:** Bruce Rolff, **Art: Dave Pratt. Yr2_OB Alamy Images:** Scott Tilley, **Art: Dave Pratt. Yr2_OB Shutterstock.com:** Giedriius, **Art: Dave Pratt,** *The Titanic*, *The Arctic Fox*, *Horrible Hiccups*, *The Night of the Bear* © Pearson Canada. Reprinted (or adapted) with permission.

All other images © Pearson Education

Every effort has been made to contact copyright holders of material reproduced in this book. Any omissions will be rectified in subsequent printings if notice is given to the publishers

Contents

An introduction to assessment

Assessment is, of course, essential and it is something that teachers do instinctively on a day-to-day basis. Because of this, assessment comes in different forms and guises. Much assessment is ongoing and **formative** as it stems from observations and informs ongoing teaching and learning in the classroom. This kind of assessment is conducted by teachers and teaching assistants, as well as by children through peer- and self-assessment. Rich questioning provides instantaneous feedback for teachers, which can result in adjustments to short- and medium-term planning. Evidence of independent practice, demonstrated in a variety of ways, also supports teachers with this type of assessment.

Summative teacher assessment also serves a purpose, both nationally and locally. While national summative assessments hold providers of education to account and provide a useful point of comparison, local summative assessments are useful in reviewing a child's ability to use and apply the knowledge and understanding they have accrued in their day-to-day learning. The Progress and Assess reading tests provide a vital insight for teachers into whether children have mastered key skills, and they also highlight where children may be having difficulty. They provide teachers with an opportunity to review what has been taught, and to plan what needs to be addressed in future lessons.

So, teaching influences assessment, and assessment influences teaching. Indeed, assessment and the curriculum are inextricably linked; all assessment should support teachers in determining how well children have understood what they have been taught, and should feed into the ongoing teaching and assessment cycle.

In all cases, assessment should be purposeful and should prompt action. Throughout the year, as we work with each child, we gain a greater and more solid understanding of their abilities, their strengths and their weaknesses. An assessment, no matter how good, is not the child. It should neither constrain our expectations nor limit our endeavours.

As such, the focus of the Progress and Assess tests and the marking guidance in this assessment guide is to provide teachers with a set of tools to help them gather and understand evidence in order to support children in their learning. The next few sections of this guide will take you through the tools we have provided.

Your reading progression maps

What are the progression maps?

This assessment guide contains a reading progression map for each of the sub-bookbands that align to National Curriculum expectations for Year 2. Children who perform well in these tests in Year 2, and who are consistently meeting the objectives in the progression maps during their everyday work in Year 2, are likely to be on track to reach their age-related expectations in reading by the end of primary school.

The progression maps track key skill areas in reading across a child's years in primary school and are designed to help you with ongoing formative assessment. They list key objectives so you can see what is expected at different stages in the school year. In order to provide teachers with a familiar frame of reference, the progression maps are linked to bookbands. So, for example, in Year 2 the expected bookband levels are Orange, Turquoise, Purple and Gold, with White and Lime intended for extension. Each bookband is divided into sub-bookbands: for example, Orange A and Orange B. This fits perfectly alongside Bug Club books, but can also be used with other reading schemes.

For children who are not yet able to work towards the Year 2 progression map objectives, progression maps for other bookbands are available in the relevant year's assessment guides and they are also available to download from ActiveLearn Primary for subscribers to either Bug Club or Progress and Assess Reading. We recommend that you assess children using the progression map that is right for the individual child, so children who are not yet working at Orange, for example, should be assessed using the progression map that corresponds to the bookband at which they are working. You can also use the progression map for the child's year group (for example, Year 2) to help you assess which skills the child needs to develop in order to get back on track, but we do not recommend that you give a child a test until they are working securely at that bookband as this can be detrimental.

For Year 2 children who are working at the expected standard, we recommend the following as a guideline for how pupils should progress through the bookbands in order to be on track to reach age-related expectations by the end of primary school.

Term 1
Children should begin to work on skills from Orange and Turquoise A, becoming more confident as the term progresses.

Term 2
Children should be secure in Turquoise A skills and should be beginning to work on skills from Turquoise B and Purple.

Term 3

Children should become secure in the skills at Gold, and could extend to White and Lime skills.

Key features of the progression maps

The progression maps have been written by an expert team of academics and teaching practitioners, including Kate Ruttle and Dee Reid, both experienced teachers, trainers and educational consultants. They ensure full coverage of all UK curricula.

The reading progression maps are broken down into skill areas and strands within them so teachers can quickly find the objectives for which they are looking. These skill areas break down the curriculum into manageable steps.

Skill Area	Strands within Skill Area
Literal Comprehension (LIT)	Literal Comprehension (LIT) Sequencing (SEQ) Information Retrieval (IR) Accuracy (ACC)
Inference (LIT)	Making Inferences (INF) Predictions (PRED)
Responding to the Text (TR)	Personal Response and Evaluation of Text (PRS) Performance (PERF)
Language for Effect (LFE)	Literary Language (LANG) Vocabulary Development (VOC)
Themes and Conventions (TAC)	Range of Texts (RGE) Text Structure (STRC)

The number of objectives listed within each strand differs from year to year.

- Any objectives in bold have been taken directly from the 2014 National Curriculum for England.

- Any text not in bold represents a smaller step that helps children to build the required skills they need by the end of the year, and helps you to check their progress along the way.

- Each skill is followed by an example to help give you a clear idea of how that skill should look in the classroom at that stage in a child's progress, to help you assess whether a child has achieved the objective.

- Where an objective is tested within one of our reading tests, we include a reference to the reading progression map in the marking guidance so you can compare your formative observations with assessment results.

How to use the progression maps

We recommend you keep a copy of the reading progression map for each child in your assessment folder.

We suggest that, each time you (or your Teaching Assistant) has a guided reading session with a group, you refer to the progression map for suggested skills focuses and make notes on how children are progressing. We provide a box within each outcome cell to help you do this. You may want to insert a tick, cross or circle to indicate when an outcome has been achieved. If you use Bug Club, the updated guided reading cards will help you assess the skills listed in the progression maps.

If you already use Bug Club or another reading programme that is structured around bookbands, it will be simple to use the progression map for the appropriate bookband. If you are not currently using bookbands, the guideline year and term will help you to assess at which bookband each child is working.

Assessment during guided reading

Guided reading is the ideal opportunity for assessing reading progress using the progression maps because children are usually in groups organised by ability and the format of a guided reading session allows for opportunities to assess those elements of reading that cannot be assessed through a written test (for example, objectives relating to performance of a play or poem).

The skills you choose to assess during guided reading will partially be determined by whether the text the group is reading is fiction or non-fiction.

Ability groups for guided reading

Guided reading sessions should be grouped by ability, with each group reading at the most appropriate bookband for the children involved. You should use the progression map that is most appropriate to each group to inform your formative assessment. You may wish to use the reading tests to provide guidance on ability grouping. These groups should be fluid so children are always working at the bookband that is right for them.

The results from the reading tests should always be viewed in the context of your ongoing formative observations. We've linked each test question to an outcome on our progression map to make it easy to compare the two.

The reading tests

About the tests

The reading tests should be used to inform ongoing teaching and learning, and to support your summative judgments.

Our tests have been designed to be flexible in their use. You should give a guided reading group the test at the most appropriate bookband, when you feel they have demonstrated success in the related skills on the progression map during guided reading sessions, ideally over a number of different texts at the same reading level. The table below shows the 'expected' time for a child to take each test, if the child is on track to reach age-related expectations by the end of primary school. Children who are moving through the bookbands more quickly than expected should be given a broad range of texts on which to practise the skills for their year group, rather than moving up to the next year's work. At Year 2, the White and Lime bookbands enable this extension. Children who are taking the tests later than expected may need some intervention to help them catch up.

There are twelve tests at Year 2:

Test name	Progression map difficulty level	Expected time for child to take test (guideline)	Genre
Orange A Test	Orange A	Year 2, term 1	Fiction
Orange B Test	Orange B	Year 2, term 1	Non-fiction
Turquoise A Test	Turquoise A	Year 2, term 1	Fiction
Turquoise B Test	Turquoise B	Year 2, term 2	Fiction
Purple A Test	Purple A	Year 2, term 2	Non-fiction
Purple B Test	Purple B	Year 2, term 2	Poetry
Gold A Test	Gold A	Year 2, term 3	Fiction
Gold B Test	Gold B	Year 2, term 3	Non-fiction
White A Test	White A	Year 2 Extension	Fiction
White B Test	White B	Year 2 Extension	Non-fiction
Lime A Test	Lime A	Year 2 Extension	Fiction
Lime B Test	Lime B	Year 2 Extension	Fiction

The tests increase in difficulty within each bookband in line with Bug Club, so, for example, Orange B is more difficult than Orange A. Not every child will need to take every test: a child who scores very well in the Orange A test, for example, may be ready to take the Turquoise A test the next time you test them, skipping the Orange B test. Using the reading progression map during your guided reading sessions will help you to decide which test is the most appropriate one for the group.

Each test in Year 2 is designed to take up to 30 minutes, so it can be completed by one group of children while other groups continue with guided reading or other related reading activities.

Format of the tests

The tests at Year 2 each have ten questions.

Eight questions score I mark each and two questions score 2 marks each (making a total of I2 marks).

The questions in the Year 2 reading tests have been carefully designed to help children acquire the skills they will need in order to complete national tests, giving them the opportunity to answer a variety of question types that they will be likely to meet. However, the Progress and Assess reading tests are not intended for use as SAT practice papers, but to help with your ongoing assessment and to give children experience of answering a variety of questions.

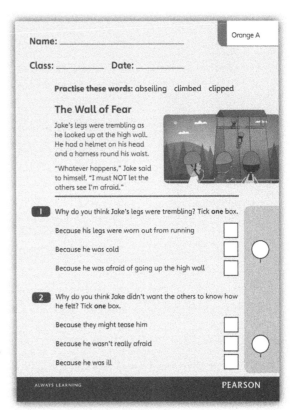

Some questions require children to tick a box or draw a line to connect information. Some questions require a one-word answer. Some questions require a longer or more considered answer (for example, sequencing events from the whole text).

Each question links directly to a skill on the reading progression map.

Supporting documents

To accompany the tests, we provide:

● marking guidance for each test. This links each question to the relevant reading progression map to help you identify each child's strengths and weaknesses (for example, a child may be secure in literal comprehension but be less confident in inferential comprehension);

- a class overview sheet that you can use to record an overview of the results from your class;

- the facilities for you to enter and track your results online, if you have a subscription to either Progress and Assess or Bug Club on ActiveLearn Primary.

Orange A Marking Guidance: The Wall of Fear
Recommended for: Year 2 Term 1

Qu.	Skill Area and Strand	Objective	Answers	Marks
1	Inference: Making Inferences Orange A/B	Participate in discussions about books they have listened to or read, making inferences about reasons for events.	Because he was afraid of going up the high wall	1
2	Inference: Making Inferences Orange A/B	Participate in discussions about books they have listened to or read, making inferences about reasons for events.	Because they might tease him	1
3	Literal Comprehension: Literal Comprehension Orange A/B	Demonstrate understanding of simple cause and effect in fiction and non-fiction texts they have read where the link between cause and effect is stated in the text and supported by a picture.	Abseil down (or similar)	1

Using the tests with your pupils

Before using the test with any group, it is important that you check you have taught the outcomes that are being assessed during your guided reading sessions. When your pupils are ready to take a test, follow the guidance below.

- Give each child the test that is the most appropriate for the bookband at which they are working. We recommend that you give children a test when they are likely to succeed in it, as giving a test that is too difficult can result in lack of confidence and will not give the child the opportunity to show what they do know.

- Ask children to write their name, class and the date at the top of the test.

- Children should work independently and should not talk to each other or be able to see each other's work. When completing prediction questions, children should use their knowledge of the text so far and not simply turn a page to find the answers. If you wish to time the test, explain that they will have 30 minutes to complete it.

- Explain that there are different types of questions that will need answering in different ways, so the children should read each question carefully. The space for their answers shows what type of answer is needed.

- A short line or a box shows that they need only write a word or a few words in their answer.
- Two or three lines shows that they need to write a longer answer.
- Some questions will require children to tick, draw lines to, or put a ring around the answer.
- Tell children that, if they run out of space on a line, they should write the rest of their answer just below.
- Remind children that, if they wish to change an answer, they should make it clear which one is correct.
- The number under each circle on the right-hand side of the page tells them the maximum number of marks for each question.
- Remind children to check their work carefully.

Marking and interpreting results

General tips

On each test there is space down the right-hand side for you to mark the tests. The number under each circle indicates the maximum number of marks for that question.

When marking the tests, it is important to refer to the appropriate marking guidance grid, provided in this guide. For pupils in your class who are not ready to take the Year 2 tests, the marking guidance documents for other tests can be found online with the appropriate test.

Once children have completed a test, it is important to identify whether there are any gaps in their knowledge or whether they have made a mistake just by being too hasty or misreading the question. Spelling mistakes in the children's answers should not affect their score for comprehension: if their meaning is understandable, accept their intended answers. The child's score will indicate whether they are on track at the expected sub-bookband.

Each test has a pass rate of 80%. Each test has been designed to assess a narrow range of ability (for example, children reading at bookband Orange A). Children who achieve 80% or more in the appropriate bookband for their year and term are on track for age-related expectations. Remember, children should be entered for tests only if you believe they can achieve the pass rate. If you do not think they can achieve this score, you should give them an easier test.

A child who scores 80% or over on a test that is two or more terms ahead of the expected test are likely to be exceeding expectations for their year and term. These children should be given the opportunity to gain a broader and deeper understanding of reading skills, for example by practising the Year 2 skills using a broader range of texts, including some free choice from the school library. At Year 2, the White and Lime bookbands enable this extension.

Test results may have an impact on guided reading groupings as some children may benefit from further work on earlier sub-bookband objectives (for example, Orange A), while others have shown they are ready for more advanced sub-bookband objectives (for example, Orange B).

How to use the marking guidance documents

A marking guidance document is provided to accompany each test. As well as providing the answers and marks for each test, and linking each question to the relevant objective on the reading progression map, these documents include two further sections that you may find useful to help you interpret children's responses.

- The 'Possible errors' column will help you to identify misconceptions and skills that children may not have mastered.

- The 'Advice' section gives advice on what to do next to help children to acquire these skills. This is addressed to the child so you can easily copy the relevant advice into the feedback section on the test paper and share with the child what they can do to improve.

Marks	Possible Errors	Advice
1	Another reason why Jake's legs might tremble, but not connected with the story	Re-read this page. What reason can you find in the story to explain why Jake was trembling?
1	An answer that's not connected with how Jake feels	Think about how Jake feels. What might happen if the other children knew how he felt?
1	Try not to think	Re-read the story on this page. What did Jake have to do?
	Have a rope clipped to his harness	Remember that in a test such as this, the questions are about the words you have just read, not about the next bit.

Understanding attainment

When you enter a child's scores into ActiveLearn Primary, the child will be given one of the following results.

Exceeding age-related expectations

The child has demonstrated a deep understanding of the required skills by getting at least 80% in a test one or more bookbands ahead of the expected one.

On track

The child is on track to achieve age-related expectations by the end of primary school and has scored at least 80% in the expected test for their year and term.

Working towards age-related expectations

The child is not currently on track, but has demonstrated some of the necessary knowledge and skills for their year and term. Children who get this result may need some short-term, targeted intervention to help them to catch up.

Below age-related expectations

The child is working significantly below the level expected for his or her age group. Children with this result may have some serious misconceptions and are likely to need intervention to help them to progress.

Unsuitably easy

The child has taken a test below the expected bookband for their year and term and has scored at least 80%. We recommend you try a harder test.

Unsuitably hard

The child has taken a test above the expected bookband for their year and term and has scored below 80%. We recommend you try an easier test.

Feeding back to children

Feeding back to children is an important part of the assessment cycle. You can record individual marks and feedback in the space provided at the end of each test.

Remember to provide feedback on what children did well, as well as areas they can improve. Make learning targets specific and achievable, and ensure you have a plan in place to support children with strengthening and extending their learning. You may find the 'Advice' section of the marking guidance document helpful when writing feedback for the child.

Feedback can take place during a guided reading session, where children can see how their peers tackled different questions. Encourage children to explain how they worked out answers to different questions.

Discussing errors can help children see where they went wrong. You may wish to share the 'Advice' section in the marking guidance document with them during a guided reading session.

For teacher use	
Your mark	_____ out of 10
What went well	
How to improve	

Class overview sheet

Class or group name: _____ Year and term: _____ Date: _____

Children's names	Test taken	Mark	Next steps
Next steps for class or group			

Child's Name _____

Skill area	Strand	Objective	
Literal Comprehension (LIT)	**Literal Comprehension (LIT)**	Demonstrate understanding of simple cause and effect in fiction and non-fiction texts they have read where the link between cause and effect is stated in the text and supported by a picture. Example: Child can explain why polar bears are suited to living in a cold climate, when the text says: 'Polar bears have thick fur which helps to keep them warm.'	
	Literal Comprehension: Sequencing (SEQ)	Refer to the book to retell main points in the correct sequence. Example: With prompting, child can summarise a simple story including main events, problem and resolution (though not necessarily using this terminology).	
	Information Retrieval (IR)		
	Accuracy (ACC)	With support, check the text makes sense as they read and correct inaccurate reading. Example: Child mis-reads 'The cat licked her paw' as 'The cat liked her paw,' and, when adult reads the sentence back with the wrong word, child recognises there is a mistake and corrects it.	
Inference (INF)	**Making Inferences (INF)**	Participate in discussions about books they have listened to or read, making inferences about reasons for events. Example: In Little Red Riding Hood, why did the wolf put on Grandma's clothes? Child answers: 'So Little Red Riding Hood would think he was Grandma.'	
	Prediction (PRED)		
Responding to the Text (RT)	**Personal Response and Evaluation of Text (PRS)**	Give a personal opinion about an event or character and give a simple justification in a discussion about a story. Example: Child can answer questions such as: 'Do you think Emma is nice?' Child answers: 'Yes' and, when asked why, adds: 'Because she helps the kitten find its mum.'	
	Performance (PERF)	Recite two or three short poems by heart, with some prompts. Example: Child is able to recite a favourite poem, remembering most of the words and with some prompts from the teacher for forgotten lines.	
Language for Effect (LFE)	**Literary Language (LANG)**	Recognise repetition of words or phrases in a short passage of text, even when that repetition is relatively subtle. Example: Child can recognise the repetition in passages such as: 'Monday was a bad day. Wednesday was a worse day. Saturday was the worst day of all.'	
	Vocabulary Development (VOC)	Able to find a word in a sentence that has the same meaning as a given word or phrase. Example: Child can find a word on the page that means that same as 'good,' e.g. 'excellent.'	
Themes and Conventions (TAC)	**Range of Texts (RGE)**	Experience and respond to different types of books, e.g. story books, factual/real-world books, rhyming and non-rhyming stories, realistic and fantasy stories. Example: Child can talk about simple non-fiction books and rhymes, as well as about story books at an appropriate level.	
	Text Structure (STRC)	Beginning to recognise that some non-fiction books have features that are different from the main text. Example: When asked to find the bit of text that tells you what the picture shows, child is able to point to a caption or label.	

16

 Works with Bug Club
Bug Club

Child's Name _____

Skill area	Strand	Objective	
Literal Comprehension (LIT)	Literal Comprehension (LIT)	Answer literal or deductive questions about books they have listened to or read, drawing on what they already know, or on background information and vocabulary provided by teacher.	
		Example: In a book about Robin Hood, child can identify that the story is set in the past and can point out some details in the story that are different from the present time.	
		Participate in discussions about books they have listened to or read, answering literal questions and making reference to significant events and characters.	
		Example: As part of a group discussion, child can name a significant event and explain how one event leads to or affects another, e.g. explaining that the three bears went out, so Goldilocks was able to get into their house.	
	Literal Comprehension: Sequencing (SEQ)	Retell, without visual prompts, recently read stories in correct sequence, in response to questions and including approximately four events.	
		Example: Child can answer questions such as: 'What happened in the beginning?,' 'What did Jack do next?,' 'What happened after that?' and 'What happened in the end?'	
	Information Retrieval (IR)		
	Accuracy (ACC)	With occasional support, check text makes sense as they read, and able to correct mistakes.	
		Example: Child mis-reads 'The dog stared at the moon' as 'The dog starred at the moon,' and, when asked to look again at the sentence, recognises it doesn't make sense and then re-reads it correctly.	
Inference (INF)	Making Inferences (INF)	Participate in discussions about books they have listened to or read, making inferences about how characters feel.	
		Example: In Hansel and Gretel, how did Hansel and Gretel feel when they first saw the gingerbread house? Child answers: 'They were excited because they were so hungry, and they probably also thought someone kind might live there, who could help them.'	
		Demonstrate understanding of simple cause and effect in fiction and non-fiction texts where the link between cause and effect is strongly implied.	
		Example: In The Fox and the Crow, what did the fox do that was clever? Child answers: 'It was clever of the fox to ask the crow to sing, because he knew that the crow would have to open her mouth and drop the cheese and he could eat it.'	
	Prediction (PRED)	Make a sensible prediction of what might happen in a text they have not encountered before and, with support, can justify the prediction on the basis of what has happened so far in the story.	
		Example: In The Boy Who Cried Wolf, child can respond to a detailed and supportive question, e.g. 'Do you think the villagers will believe him this third time?' Child says: 'No' and, when prompted, justifies response, e.g. 'Because they will think he is making it up again.'	
Responding to the Text (RT)	Personal Response and Evaluation of Text (PRS)	Explain how a story, poem or non-fiction topic makes them feel.	
		Example: After listening to a poem, child is able to answer the question: 'How did the poem make you feel?' Child answers: 'It made me feel sad.'	
		With support, form a simple question they would like to ask a character about events from the story.	
		Example: After hearing some modelled questions to ask Little Red Riding Hood, child can ask: 'Why did you think the wolf was your Grandma?'	
	Performance (PERF)	Recite with accuracy about three familiar short poems by heart.	
		Example: Child is able to recite a favourite poem from a choice of three that they know, remembering all of the words with very few or no prompts.	

17

Child's Name _____

Language for Effect (LFE)	**Literary Language (LANG)**	Recognise clear patterns of language, such as the repetition of words or phrases. Example: When reading Jack and the Beanstalk, child can answer the question: 'What will the giant say when he comes back to the castle the third time.' Child can use their knowledge of what the giant said the first two times to answer: 'Fee fi fo fum…'	
		With support, sometimes identify specific examples of literary language in texts they have listened to or read, e.g. alliteration. Example: When asked: 'How has the author made the description sound special?' child can sometimes pick out an example of alliteration or other literary language.	
	Vocabulary Development (VOC)	Able to find a word in a page of text that has the same meaning as a given word. Example: When asked to find a word that means 'jumped' in a page of text, child can point out the word 'leaped.'	
Themes and Conventions (TAC)	**Range of Texts (RGE)**	Contribute appropriately to discussion about a wide range of different types of texts they have listened to or read, including stories, traditional tales, poems and non-fiction. Example: Child can add an appropriate comment to a discussion about a non-fiction text by picking up on an aspect of the text that relates to their own experience or by relating something interesting they learned from the text.	
	Text Structure (STRC)	Know what some common non-fiction features are called and what they do. Example: When asked to point to a caption, child can point to a caption on a page and, when asked, can explain that it tells you about the picture.	
		With support, clearly explain what some common non-fiction features are called and what they do. Example: When asked which part of the text tells you what is in the picture, child says 'a label', and points to a label.	

18

Works with Bug Club

Bug Club

Pearson Primary Progress and Assess
Reading Progression Map

Year 2, term 2
Purple

Child's Name _____

Skill area	Strand	Objective	
Literal Comprehension (LIT)	**Literal Comprehension (LIT)**	Answer literal questions about books they have listened to or read, using new vocabulary they have met in the text. Example: In a non-fiction book about how chocolate is made, child can answer questions using words and phrases such as 'cacao tree' or 'chocolate moulds'.	
	Literal Comprehension: Sequencing (SEQ)	Retell recently read stories, including main characters and most key events, in correct order with minimal prompting. Example: In Jack and the Beanstalk, child can say that Jack went up a beanstalk, ran back down the beanstalk and then chopped it down. Teacher asks: 'What was at the top of the beanstalk?' and child can answer.	
	Information Retrieval (IR)		
	Accuracy (ACC)	Usually checks for themselves that text makes sense as they read, and correct inaccurate reading. Example: Child mis-reads 'The lion wouldn't stop roaring' as 'The lion would stop roaring,' recognises it doesn't make sense and self-corrects, and usually does this unprompted.	
Inference (INF)	**Making Inferences (INF)**	Participate in discussions about books they have listened or read, making simple inferences on the basis of what characters do. Example: In Robin Hood, why did Robin Hood steal from rich people and give to poor people?' Child answers: 'The poor people were starving and Robin Hood wanted to help them.'	
	Prediction (PRED)		
Responding to the Text (RT)	**Personal Response and Evaluation of Text (PRS)**	With some support, explain and discuss their understanding of books, poems and other material in simple terms. Example: After listening to a poem, child is able to answer the questions: 'How did the poem make you feel?' Child answers: 'It made me feel sad.' With prompting, child can explain why in very simple terms, e.g. 'Because the girl in the poem is sad.'	
	Performance (PERF)	Recite about four poems by heart, and beginning to use appropriate intonation to make the meaning clear. Example: When reciting a poem, child uses appropriate intonation for some questions or exclamations, but may not do this consistently.	
Language for Effect (LFE)	**Literary Language (LANG)**	Recognise rhymes or alliteration in poems they have listened to or read. Example: After listening to a poem, teacher asks: 'Which word has the poet used to rhyme with "rain"?' and then re-reads the relevant lines. Child is able to answer 'drain.'	
	Vocabulary Development (VOC)	Identify their favourite words and phrases. Example: When looking at or listening to a short poem, child is able to point out words and phrases that appeal to them.	
Themes and Conventions (TAC)	**Range of Texts (RGE)**		
	Text Structure (STRC)	Able to read non-fiction texts that include one or more common non-fiction features and can tell you what some features are called. Example: Child can read aloud a page of an unfamiliar non-fiction text that includes a caption or label and can name these features.	

19

 **Works with Bug Club**
Bug Club

Child's Name _____

Skill area	Strand	Objective	
Literal Comprehension (LIT)	**Literal Comprehension (LIT)**	Participate in discussions about books they have listened to or read, recalling the story and making reference to significant events and characters.	
		Example: As part of a group discussion, child can recall significant events and explain why they were important in the story, e.g. the ship was burning, so the pirate jumped into the sea and swam to the island, but there was a dragon there.	
		Ask and answer questions about books they have listened to or read, often making links between one event or piece of information and another, and where necessary drawing on what they already know or on background information and vocabulary provided by the teacher.	
		Example: When reading a story about two friends having an argument, child can ask and answer questions that help them make the connection between one of the character's behaviour towards the other, and what happens next.	
	Literal Comprehension: Sequencing (SEQ)	Become increasingly familiar with wider range of stories, fairy stories and traditional tales and can retell these.	
		Example: Child can retell a range of familiar stories, including main characters and key events in the correct order, e.g. child can summarise Cinderella, briefly describing Cinderella's life, how she got to the ball, what happened at the ball and what happened after that.	
		Demonstrate understanding of simple cause and effect in fiction and non-fiction texts, discussing sequence of events and explaining how items of information are related.	
		Example: When discussing Little Red Riding Hood, child can answer questions such as: 'What was the wolf's plan?' (He would put on Grandma's clothes so that Little Red Riding Hood would think he was Grandma and then he could eat Little Red Riding Hood).	
	Information Retrieval (IR)	With support, find specific information on a page of non-fiction text, often using features such as key words, headings, captions, etc. appropriately.	
		Example: With support, child can answer question such as: 'Can you explain where swallows go in the winter?'	
	Accuracy (ACC)	Independently check text makes sense as they read, and correct inaccurate reading.	
		Example: Child mis-reads 'The knight ran into the palace' as 'The knight ran into the place,' realises it doesn't make sense, and self-corrects without being prompted.	
Inference (INF)	**Making Inferences (INF)**	Discuss why some events in a story are important and make simple links between items of information.	
		Example: When discussing a non-fiction book about how rice is grown, child can answer questions such as: 'Why do you think we don't grow much rice in the UK?' (Because our climate isn't ideal for growing rice, and it would take up a lot of land that we could better use for other things.)	
		Participate in discussions about books they have listened or read, making inferences on the basis of what is said and done and listening to what others say.	
		Example: In Sinbad the Sailor, how did the sailors feel when they saw the pile of bones? Child answers: 'The sailors were scared that something bad might happen to them'.	
	Prediction (PRED)	Make a sensible prediction of what might happen and, when prompted, justify the prediction on the basis of what has happened so far in the story.	
		Example: In The Boy Who Cried Wolf (when this is unfamiliar to child), when the boy sees the wolf, child can answer more open and less supportive questions, e.g. 'What will the villagers say?' (They will say he is lying) and 'Why do you think that?' (Because he had lied about it before).	
Responding to the Text (RT)	**Personal Response and Evaluation of Text (PRS)**	With support, use empathy to help them understand characters and their motivation.	
		Example: Following a spoken example, child can ask a question such as: 'Why did you choose the dragon as a pet?' When in the hot seat, child can give a simple, appropriate answer, e.g. 'Because it was friendly.'	
		Explain and discuss their understanding of books, poems and other material they have listened to or read, sometimes giving a more detailed account of their opinions.	
		Example: After listening to a poem, child gives a personal response to the question: 'How did the poem make you feel?' Child answers: 'It made me feel sad.' With prompting, child can explain why in simple terms, e.g. 'Because the girl in the poem is lonely, and I felt sorry for her.'	
	Performance (PERF)	Recite at least five poems by heart, adding appropriate intonation to make the meaning clear.	
		Example: When reciting a poem, child quickens their pace or uses an excited tone of voice for an exciting part of the poem.	

20

Works with Bug Club
Bug Club

Child's Name _____

Language for Effect (LFE)	**Literary Language (LANG)**	Recognise interesting vocabulary in a text they have listened to or read.	
		Example: When asked: 'Which word has the author used to help us imagine how loudly the baby was crying?' child can respond with the word 'wailed.'	
		Recognise simple recurring literary language in stories and poetry.	
		Example: Child can find examples of alliteration or simple figurative language in a text, when the text contains numerous examples of this kind of language.	
	Vocabulary Development (VOC)	Discuss their favourite words and phrases.	
		Example: When looking at a page of text, child is able to point out words and phrases that appeal to them and explain in simple terms why they like these words, e.g. for the word 'spooky' child says 'I like it because it sounds scary.'	
		Discuss and clarify the meanings of words, linking new meanings to known vocabulary.	
		Example: When child comes across a new word such as 'shattered,' they are able to make a sensible guess at the meaning using the context and can suggest an alternative word that could be used, e.g. 'broken.'	
Themes and Conventions (TAC)	**Range of Texts (RGE)**	Discuss and express views about a wide range of texts they have listened to.	
		Example: Child is able to discuss how they would feel in a character's place in stories; how poems make them feel and what they think of topics discussed in non-fiction texts.	
	Text Structure (STRC)	With support, can sometimes comment on the appropriateness of the author's choice of title for a poem or story.	
		Example: When asked why a title might be a good choice for a story or poem, child can make some link between the title and the content of the writing.	
		Able to read a range of non-fiction texts structured in different ways.	
		Example: Child can read a range of texts including simple instructions, books with non-fiction features such as captions and labels and simple online texts.	

21

Orange A Marking Guidance: The Wall of Fear

Recommended for: Year 2 Term 1

Qu.	Skill Area and Strand	Objective	Answers	Marks	Possible Errors	Advice
1	Inference: Making Inferences Orange A/B	Participate in discussions about books they have listened to or read, making inferences about reasons for events.	Because he was afraid of going up the high wall	1	Another reason why Jake's legs might tremble, but not connected with the story	Re-read this page. What reason can you find in the story to explain why Jake was trembling?
2	Inference: Making Inferences Orange A/B	Participate in discussions about books they have listened to or read, making inferences about reasons for events.	Because they might tease him	1	An answer that's not connected with how Jake feels	Think about how Jake feels. What might happen if the other children knew how he felt?
3	Literal Comprehension: Literal Comprehension Orange A/B	Demonstrate understanding of simple cause and effect in fiction and non-fiction texts they have read where the link between cause and effect is stated in the text and supported by a picture.	Abseil down (or similar)	1	Try not to think Have a rope clipped to his harness	Re-read the story on this page. What did Jake have to do? Remember that in a test such as this, the questions are about the words you have just read, not about the next bit.
4	Language for Effect: Vocabulary Development Orange A/B	Able to find a word in a sentence that has the same meaning as a given word or phrase.	Instructor	1	Any incorrect answer	Look for one word that could mean 'a person who teaches you how to do things'. Try replacing the word with this phrase. Does the sentence still make sense?

#		Skill	Criteria	Answer	Mark	Misconception	Question
5	Literal Comprehension: Literal Comprehension Orange A/B	Demonstrate understanding of simple cause and effect in fiction and non-fiction texts they have read where the link between cause and effect is stated in the text and supported by a picture.	Afraid (or similar) But Jake was too afraid to speak.	2	Not understanding that Jake is afraid Not identifying the sentence that tells us he is afraid	How does Jake feel about going abseiling? Think of a word to describe that feeling. Jake feels afraid. Find a sentence that tells us this.
6	Language for Effect: Vocabulary Development Orange A/B	Able to find a word in a sentence that has the same meaning as a given word or phrase.	Picture of a child abseiling	1	The picture of Jake, even though he is not abseiling, or the picture of people sailing, misunderstanding the word 'abseiling'	Jake was frightened because he had to abseil down a high wall. Which picture shows Jake abseiling?
7	Literal Comprehension: Literal Comprehension Orange A/B	Demonstrate understanding of simple cause and effect in fiction and non-fiction texts they have read where the link between cause and effect is stated in the text and supported by a picture.	He wanted to show Max and Jordan he could do it.	1	Another reason that is not supported by the story	Think about what the story tells us. Who does Jake see, and what does he say?
8	Literal Comprehension: Sequencing Orange A/B	Refer to the book to retell main points in the correct sequence.	Children's own words similar to: 'he climbed the ladder to the top' and 'he abseiled down'	2	Sentences that do not convey the main things that happened in the story	Think about the main things that happened in the story. Can you write two sentences to sum up what happened on page 2 and on page 4?
				Total:	**10**		

Orange A Marking Guidance: The Wall of Fear

Orange B Marking Guidance: Wild Rabbits

Recommended for: Year 2 Term 1

Qu.	Skill Area and Strand	Objective	Answers	Marks	Possible Errors	Advice
1	Literal Comprehension: Literal Comprehension Orange A/B	Demonstrate understanding of simple cause and effect in fiction and non-fiction texts they have read where the link between cause and effect is stated in the text and supported by a picture.	They have the same sort of eyes and fur.	1	They live in the same places as pet rabbits. They have a different sort of life from pet rabbits.	This is not an explanation for how rabbits look like pet rabbits. Re-read the text. In what way do wild rabbits look like pet rabbits? This is true, but it doesn't say how they look like pet rabbits. Re-read the text and find an explanation of how wild rabbits look like pet rabbits.
2	Language for Effect: Vocabulary Development Orange A/B	Able to find a word in a sentence that has the same meaning as a given word or phrase.	Bright	1	Any incorrect answer	Try replacing the word you have chosen with 'shining' in the text. Does it still make sense?
3	Language for Effect: Vocabulary Development Orange A/B	Able to find a word in a sentence that has the same meaning as a given word or phrase.	Warren Also accept: tunnels. Some children may give 'dig' as an answer, using prior knowledge of the verb 'burrow'.	1	Any incorrect answer	The text says that rabbits dig something. What do they dig? What are these called?

24

No.	Skill	Objective	Success criteria	Mark	Misconception	Question
4	Inference: Making Inferences Orange A/B	Participate in discussions about books they have listened to or read, making inferences about reasons for events.	Accept answers that indicate the difference in size between the rabbits and their predators, such as: The rabbits are small so they can hide in the tunnels. The larger animals can't get through the tunnels.	2	Children may not be able to make the link between the size of the tunnels in relation to the rabbits' predators.	Re-read the text and look at the photo. Do you think a fox would be able to get inside this tunnel? How do you think this would help the rabbits?
5	Themes and Conventions: Text Structure Orange A/B	Beginning to recognise that some non-fiction books have features that are different from the main text.	It shows us what a warren is like inside.	1	It tells us about what rabbits eat. It gives lots of information about rabbits' nesting areas.	This page doesn't tell us about what rabbits eat. What is the page mostly about? This page mentions rabbits' nesting areas, but it doesn't give lots of information about them. What is the page mostly about?
6	Themes and Conventions: Text Structure Orange A/B	Beginning to recognise that some non-fiction books have features that are different from the main text.	Correctly identifies and circles a label (1 mark); Writes the label down correctly (1 mark)	2	Not understanding what a label is. Not writing the label correctly	Labels are words that give us more information about part of a picture. They often have an arrow or line that points to the picture. Find a label on the page, and write down exactly what it says.

7	Literal Comprehension: Literal Comprehension Orange A/B	Demonstrate understanding of simple cause and effect in fiction and non-fiction texts they have read where the link between cause and effect is stated in the text and supported by a picture.	To warn other rabbits about an enemy (or similar)	1	Another reason that is not supported by the text	Think about what the text tells us. What makes the rabbits start making a thumping noise? What happens when they do this?
8	Inference: Making Inferences Orange A/B	Participate in discussions about books they have listened to or read, making inferences about reasons for events.	So they can easily run home if an enemy comes	1	Because the grass near their home is tasty Because they like eating grass and small plants	This is not what the text tells us. Think about what happens when an enemy comes – where do the rabbits run to? It's true that they like eating grass and small plants, but this is not why they stay close to their warren. Re-read the text. What is the most likely reason why they might stay close to home?
			Total:	**10**		

Turquoise A Marking Guidance: Theseus and the Minotaur

Recommended for: Year 2 Term 1

Qu.	Skill Area and Strand	Objective	Answers	Marks	Possible Errors	Advice
1	Language for Effect: Vocabulary Development Turquoise A	Able to find a word in a page of text that has the same meaning as a given word.	Horrible	1	Difficult	'Difficult' doesn't mean the same as 'nasty'. Which word on the page means 'nasty'?
					Another word unconnected with 'nasty' in meaning	What does 'nasty' mean? Look it up in the dictionary if you need to. Then find a word that means the same as 'nasty'.
2	Literal Comprehension: Literal Comprehension Turquoise A	Answer literal or deductive questions about books they have listened to or read, drawing on what they already know, or on background information and vocabulary provided by the teacher.	Accept one of the following (or similar): in a maze; in a labyrinth; deep underground	1	A guess that doesn't draw on evidence from the story	Re-read this page. What does it tell us about where the Minotaur lives?
					Half-human, half-bull	Look at the first word in the question. 'Where' must be answered with a place. Re-read the page, thinking about the place where the minotaur lived.

3	Inferences: Making Inferences Turquoise A	Participate in discussions about books they have listened to or read, making inferences about how characters feel.	a) Accept one of the following (or similar): scared; worried (1 mark) b) Accept one of the following: He could hear his own heart beating: thump-thump, thump-thump. The string would help him find his way out after he had killed the Minotaur ... if he was still alive by then! (1 mark)	2	Not understanding what the text tells us about how Theseus feels Not identifying a sentence that gives evidence about Theseus's feelings	How do you think Theseus would feel about having to go by himself in the dark to kill a scary monster? Look for a sentence that gives us a clue about Theseus's feelings e.g., his heart is beating loudly.
4	Literal Comprehension: Literal Comprehension Turquoise A	Answer literal or deductive questions about books they have listened to or read, drawing on what they already know, or on background information and vocabulary provided by the teacher.	The string would help him to find his way out of the labyrinth.	1	The string would help him to kill the Minotaur. The string would help him to remember what he had to do.	Re-read the page. What does it tell us about the string and how it could help Theseus?
5	Language for Effect: Literary Language Turquoise A	Recognise clear patterns of language, such as the repetition of words or phrases.	Thump-thump, thump-thump	1	Faster and faster; closer and closer	This word/phrase doesn't tell us about the sound Theseus's heart was making. Look at page 3 for clues about the sound his heart made.

6	Inferences: Prediction Turquoise A	Make a sensible prediction of what might happen in a text they have not encountered before and, with support, can justify the prediction on the basis of what has happened so far in the story.	a) Accept any answer that makes a reasonable prediction (1 mark)	2	Not able to make a prediction or justify it	Think about what is most likely to happen next. Will Theseus meet the Minotaur? Will they fight? Think about what happens in other stories you know that are a bit like this one.
			b) Accept any answer that attempts to justify the prediction (1 mark)		Making a prediction that is not justified by the text	That doesn't sound as if it is very likely to happen in this story. Think about what might happen when Theseus and the Minotaur meet.
7	Language for Effect: Vocabulary Development Turquoise A	Able to find a word in a page of text that has the same meaning as a given word.	Grabbed	1	Twisted	'Twisted' doesn't mean exactly the same as 'took hold of', because you can take hold of something without twisting it. Which word means the same as 'took hold of'?
					Another word unconnected with 'took hold of' in meaning	Think about what 'took hold of' means. Which word in the story means the same as 'took hold of'?

8	Responding to the Text: Personal Response and Evaluation of Text Turquoise A	Explain how a story, poem or non-fiction topic makes them feel.	Accept any answer that shows an emotional response to this particular story, such as: happy (that Theseus is safe); excited (by the action of the story); sad / sorry (for the Minotaur)	1	An answer that doesn't express an emotional response to the story. Children may describe what happens rather than saying how this made them feel.	Think about what happens at the end. Does Theseus win against the Minotaur? How does it make you feel?
		Total:		**10**		

Turquoise B Marking Guidance: Sasha's Diary

Recommended for: Year 2 Term 2

Qu.	Skill Area and Strand	Objective	Answers	Marks	Possible Errors	Advice
1	Literal Comprehension: Literal Comprehension Turquoise B	Participate in discussions about books they have listened to or read, answering literal questions and making reference to significant events and characters.	Near the sea	1	Any incorrect answer Children may not read the text carefully.	Re-read this page. Where does Sasha tell us their tent was?
2	Inference: Making Inferences Turquoise B	Demonstrate understanding of simple cause and effect in fiction and non-fiction texts where the link between cause and effect is strongly implied.	a) Mum and Dad (1 mark) b) Because it was raining when they put the tent up (1 mark)	2	Some children may not read the caption, or understand the word 'soaked' in the question. Children may not link pieces of information together (it was raining and therefore Mum and Dad got very wet).	Look at the caption to the picture. Who got wet? What were they doing? What was the weather like when they put the tent up?
3	Language for Effect: Literary Language Turquoise B	With support, sometimes identify specific examples of literary language in texts they have listened to or read, e.g. alliteration.	Swishing; swooshing Also accept either of these plus 'lovely'	1	Other words from the passage	What sounds does Sasha hear the sea making? Write down the words she uses to describe it.

No.	Strand	Objective	Answer	Marks	Possible misconceptions	Question
4	Themes and Conventions: Text Structure Turquoise B	With support, clearly explain what some common non-fiction features are called and what they do.	a) Dad was a bit cross when he woke up! (1 mark) b) Captions give the reader more information about a picture (1 mark).	2	Some children may not understand which part of the text is the caption. Some children may not understand or remember what a caption is for.	Look at the picture. A caption is a sentence or phrase that gives extra information about a picture. Look at the caption. What information does it add to the picture? Think about why captions might be useful.
5	Literal Comprehension: Literal Comprehension Turquoise B	Participate in discussions about books they have listened to or read, answering literal questions and making reference to significant events and characters.	Jack and Sasha	1	Some children may answer Jack, Sasha and Mum, if referring to the image, and not understanding the difference between paddling and swimming.	Re-read page 3. Who was stood on the beach? Who went swimming, and who didn't?
6	Inference: Making Inferences Turquoise B	Demonstrate understanding of simple cause and effect in fiction and non-fiction texts where the link between cause and effect is strongly implied.	The wave nearly knocked her over.	1	Some children may not understand what happened to Mum on this page, or look at the caption.	Re-read the text and caption on page 3. What happened to Mum while she was paddling? Why do you think she nearly fell over?
7	Inference: Making Inferences Turquoise B	Demonstrate understanding of simple cause and effect in fiction and non-fiction texts where the link between cause and effect is strongly implied.	Because she had enjoyed camping and she was sorry it was time to go home (or similar)	1	An answer that indicates the child has not understood Sasha's feelings	Did Sasha enjoy camping? How do you think she felt when it was time to go home?

8	Literal Comprehension: Literal Comprehension Turquoise B	Participate in discussions about books they have listened to or read, answering literal questions and making reference to significant events and characters.	They put the tent pegs away.	1	An answer that doesn't reflect the text	Re-read page 4. What does Sasha tell us that she and Jack did to help?

Total: 10

Purple A Marking Guidance: The Titanic

Recommended for: Year 2 Term 2

Qu.	Skill Area and Strand	Objective	Answers	Marks	Possible Errors	Advice
1	Inference: Making Inferences Purple A/B	Participate in discussions about books they have listened to or read, making simple inferences.	Because it looked very beautiful and expensive	1	Because it was made of gold	This isn't what the text tells us about the *Titanic*. Re-read the text. What did the *Titanic* look like?
					Because it always stayed afloat	This doesn't explain why people said it was like a palace. Why might they have compared it to a palace?
2	Literal Comprehension: Literal Comprehension Purple A/B	Answer literal questions about books they have listened to or read, using new vocabulary they have met in the text.	Accept any two of the following (or similar): It was the largest ship ever built. It looked beautiful. Its owners said it was the safest ship in the world. (Award 1 mark for each special characteristic given.)	2	Only one special characteristic given	Look for another thing that the text tells us was special about the *Titanic*.
					A guess not related to the text or question	Re-read the text. Look for two things that made people think the *Titanic* was special.

34

3	Literal Comprehension: Literal Comprehension Purple A/B	Answer literal questions about books they have listened to or read, using new vocabulary they have met in the text.	If one layer got damaged, the second layer would still keep out the water. (Or similar appropriate answer)	1	Some children may not understand what the double hull was, and how it was meant to work.	Look for part of the text that tells us how the double hull was meant to work.
4	Literal Comprehension: Literal Comprehension Purple A/B	Answer literal questions about books they have listened to or read, using new vocabulary they have met in the text.	New York	1	Some children may get confused about which is the start and which is the end destination as both are mentioned in the text. Atlanta may be confused with Atlantic Ocean if children are scanning the text for a match.	Re-read the text. Where did the *Titanic* start out from? Where was it going to?
5	Literal Comprehension: Literal Comprehension Purple A/B	Answer literal questions about books they have listened to or read, using new vocabulary they have met in the text.	More than 1500	1	Any incorrect answer	Re-read the text on page 3. What does it tell us about the number of people who died?

6	Themes and Conventions: Text Structure Purple A/B Able to read non-fiction texts that include one or more common non-fiction features and can tell you what some features are called.	The *Titanic* hit an iceberg like this one. (Or similar appropriate caption) (Award 1 mark for understanding what a caption is. Award 1 mark for writing an appropriate caption.)	2	Writing a label (single word or short phrase) Writing a caption that doesn't go with this picture or relate to the *Titanic*	A caption is normally a sentence that tells us something more about a picture. Write a caption that goes with this picture. Think about what the picture shows, and what the question tells us about the iceberg in the picture. Write a caption that uses this information.
7	Literal Comprehension: Sequencing Purple A/B Retell recently read texts, including most key events, in correct order with minimal prompting.	1. The *Titanic* set sail from Southampton. 2. The *Titanic* hit an iceberg. 3. The *Titanic* sank very fast. 4. Scientists travelled down to look at the wreck. 5. Scientists worked out what had happened to the *Titanic*.	1	Getting the sequence wrong	Re-read the text. Think about the order in which things happened.
8	Literal Comprehension: Literal Comprehension Purple A/B Answer literal questions about books they have listened to or read, using new vocabulary they have met in the text.	They went down in a mini-submarine. (Or similar appropriate answer)	1	Answer that doesn't reflect the text	Re-read the text on page 4. What does it tell us about how the scientists travelled down to the wreck?
		Total:	**10**		

Purple B Marking Guidance: Space Adventure

Recommended for: Year 2 Term 2

Qu.	Skill Area and Strand	Objective	Answers	Marks	Possible Errors	Advice
1	Inferences: Making Inferences Purple A/B	Participate in discussions about books they have listened to or read, making simple inferences on the basis of what characters do.	Because he doesn't know what he is going to find in space (Or similar appropriate answer)	1	A guess not related to the text	Think about what the text tells us about why the astronaut is feeling scared. What does he say about it?
2	Language for Effect: Vocabulary Development Purple A/B	Identify their favourite words and phrases.	Growl; roar (Award 1 mark for each word.)	2	Other words not connected with the sound of the engines	Think about how the text describes the sound of the engines. What words does the author use?
3	Literal Comprehension: Literal Comprehension Purple A/B	Answer literal questions about books they have listened to or read, using new vocabulary they have met in the text.	Asteroids	1	A guess not connected with the text	Re-read the text. What does it tell us about what the astronaut sees out of the window?
4	Inference: Making Inferences Purple A/B	Participate in discussions about books they have listened to or read, making simple inferences on the basis of what characters do.	He hopes the rocket can fly around the asteroids without hitting them.	1	Any incorrect answer	Re-read the text. What is happening when the astronaut says, 'I hope the rocket swerves'?

	Objective	Answer	Mark		Question
5	Literal Comprehension: Literal Comprehension Purple A/B	Answer literal questions about books they have listened to or read, using new vocabulary they have met in the text.	The asteroids have damaged it.	1	Any incorrect answer	This isn't the problem that the text tells us about. What problem is mentioned in the text?
6	Language for Effect: Literary Language Purple A/B	Recognise rhymes or alliteration in poems they have listened to or read.	Sight	1	Alternative word that doesn't rhyme	Words that rhyme have the same sound at the end. Which word on the page rhymes with 'white'?
7	Literal Comprehension: Sequencing Purple A/B	Retell recently read stories, including main characters and most key events, in correct order with minimal prompting.	Next, the rocket took off. Then the rocket landed on a planet. (Or similar appropriate answers) (Award 1 mark for each correct sentence.)	2	Answers that do not show an understanding of the sequence of events	Re-read the text. Think about what happened and when.
8	Responding to the Text: Personal Response and Evaluation of the Text Purple A/B	With some support, explain and discuss their understanding of books, poems and other material in simple terms.	Accept any answer that relates to something that might be surprising. For example: that the astronaut turns out to be an alien, or that human children help him to mend his rocket.	1	An answer that doesn't include something surprising	Read the poem again. Did anything in the poem surprise you? Did you think it was surprising that the astronaut was an alien, and the 'aliens' turned out to be humans?

Total: 10

Gold A Marking Guidance: Spiders and Flies: An Eritrean Story

Recommended for: Year 2 Term 3

Qu.	Skill Area and Strand	Objective	Answers	Marks	Possible Errors	Advice
1	Literal Comprehension: Literal Comprehension Gold A	Participate in discussions about books they have listened to or read, making reference to significant events and characters.	They are ugly. They do no work. (Award 1 mark for each reason.)	2	Just one reason given	This is one reason why the prince didn't like spiders and flies. Can you find another one?
					Reasons that are not in the text	Re-read the story on page 1. What two things did the prince say about spiders and flies to explain why he didn't like them?
2	Language for Effect: Literary Language Gold A	Recognise interesting vocabulary in a text they have listened to or read.	Softly	1	Another word not related to how the queen spoke	Look for a word in the story that describes how the queen spoke.
					Another word not in the text	This word isn't in the story – find a word in the story to describe how the queen spoke.
3	Inference: Making Inferences Gold A	Discuss why some events in a story are important and make simple links between items of information.	All of his family were killed in the war. The prince's enemies were after him. (Or similar appropriate answer)	1	A guess not connected with the text	Re-read the text. What does it tell us about what happened before the prince decided to go and live with his uncle?

Gold A Marking Guidance: Spiders and Flies: An Eritrean Story

4	Responding to the Text: Personal Response and Evaluation of Text Gold A	With support, use empathy to help them understand characters and their motivation.	Upset and worried	1	Any incorrect answer	Think about what has just happened – all the prince's family have been killed. How do you think he might feel?
5	Inference: Making Inferences Gold A	Discuss why some events in a story are important and make simple links between items of information.	Because he had the chance to see his enemies coming and was able to run away (Or similar appropriate answer)	1	Answer that shows the child hasn't understood why this event is significant	Think about what would have happened if the prince hadn't woken up then. Would his enemies have found him?

No.	Objective	Correct answer	Marks	Incorrect	Question
6	Inference: Prediction Gold A	Make a sensible prediction of what might happen and, when prompted, justify the prediction on the basis of what has happened so far in the story.	a) The spider might help the prince to hide from his enemies. b) Because the prince has just been helped by a fly, so now I think a spider will help him (Or another plausible prediction supported by reasons related to the text) (Award 1 mark for prediction, and 1 mark for justification)	2	Prediction that doesn't fit with the story so far No justification given for prediction	Think about the story so far. What do you think is likely to happen to the prince next? Will his enemies find him? Will the spider help him to escape somehow? Think about what has happened so far in the story. How does this help to explain what might happen next?
7	Literal Comprehension: Literal Comprehension Gold A	Participate in discussions about books they have listened to or read, making reference to significant events and characters.	Because they thought the spider's web showed that no one had gone into the cave recently	1	Any incorrect answer	Think about what the man says about the spider's web. What does he think it means?

8	Inference: Making Inferences Gold A	Discuss why some events in a story are important and make simple links between items of information.	No. A spider and fly helped him to escape from his enemies, so the prince has likely changed his mind about them. (Or similar appropriate answer)	1	An answer that doesn't reflect the fact that the prince's views on spiders and flies are likely to have changed	How did the prince feel about spiders and flies at the start of the story? How did a fly and a spider help him? Do you think this might stop the prince moaning about spiders and flies?
			Total:	10		

Gold B Marking Guidance: The Arctic Fox

Recommended for: Year 2 Term 3

Qu.	Skill Area and Strand	Objective	Answers	Marks	Possible Errors	Advice
1	Literal Comprehension: Literal Comprehension Gold B	Answer questions, making links between one event or piece of information and another.	Canada	1	In a den Another country where Arctic foxes might be found	Read the questions carefully, looking for key words (e.g. 'country'). When answering a comprehension question, look for information in the text.
2	Literal Comprehension: Literal Comprehension Gold B	Answer questions, making links between one event or piece of information and another.	Brown	1	White	Read the text carefully, taking care to choose the most useful piece of information. You might have to connect information from two sentences to find an answer.
3	Language for Effect: Vocabulary Development Gold B	Clarify the meanings of words, linking new meanings to known vocabulary.	Paws	1	Ears; tail; coat	Look for familiar parts of words as a clue to the meaning (e.g. 'foot').
4	Literal Comprehension: Literal Comprehension Gold B	Answer questions, making links between one event or piece of information and another.	They are both bushy.	1	It protects it from the cold.	Make sure you choose the right bit of information to answer the question.
5	Inference: Making Inferences Gold B	Making inferences on the basis of what is said and done.	It can hear small animals under the snow.	1	It has small ears. It eats berries. It lives underground.	Read the question carefully and look for clues in the text.

Gold B Marking Guidance: The Arctic Fox

No.	Objective	Answer	Marks		Tips
6	Literal Comprehension: Sequencing Gold B	Demonstrate understanding of simple cause and effect in non-fiction texts, explaining how items of information are related.	It keeps the Arctic fox warm. It makes it hard for enemies to see the Arctic fox in the snow. (Award 1 mark for each correct answer.)	2	It makes it hard for enemies to see the Arctic fox on the rocky ground. It turns brown. It has fur on its footpads.	Read the question carefully and make sure you are looking at the right part of the text. Look at the 'question word' to understand what it is asking you (e.g. 'how', not 'what' or 'where').
7	Literal Comprehension: Literal Comprehension Gold B	Answer questions, making links between one event or piece of information and another.	Accept any four of the following: small animals; mice; meat; birds; fish; birds' eggs; berries; leftover food; droppings (Award 1 mark for two or three correct answers. Award 2 marks for four correct answers.)	2	Wolves; polar bears. Some children may give fewer than four answers.	Read the text carefully. Read the instructions carefully and fill in all of the answer lines.
8	Themes and Conventions: Text Structure Gold B	Able to read a range of non-fiction texts structured in different ways.	Thick; white (Award 1 mark for getting both correct, in either order.)	1	Brown; thin White; white Thick; thick	Read the question carefully and don't just copy from the labels given. Read the instructions carefully ('two different words').
			Total:	10		

White A Marking Guidance: Mr Shenks and Lancelot

Recommended for: Year 2 Extension

Qu.	Skill Area and Strand	Objective	Answers	Marks	Possible Errors	Advice
1	Literal Comprehension: Literal Comprehension White A/B	Participate in discussions about books they have listened to or read, recalling the story and making reference to significant events and characters.	He lives on their road.	1	Any incorrect answer	Re-read the story on this page. What does it tell us about Mr Shenks? Why might the girls recognise him?
2	Inference: Making Inferences White A/B	Participate in discussions about books they have listened to or read, making inferences on the basis of what is said and done, and listening to what others say.	Accept any two of the following: He is acting in a way that makes him seem like a spy. He is looking in bushes. The girls have just been watching a spy film, so they are thinking about spies. (Award 1 mark for each reason, up to 2 marks.)	2	Not finding two reasons in the text / Made-up reason/s that are not justified by the text	Re-read the story on this page. Can you find another reason why the girls might think Mr Shenks is a spy? What might a spy do? Why are the girls thinking about spies at the moment? Re-read the story on this page. Look for evidence about how Mr Shenks is acting, and think about why the girls might be thinking of spies at the moment.

#	Strand	Objective	Accept	Marks	Do not accept	Question
3	Inference: Prediction White A/B	Make a sensible prediction of what might happen and, when prompted, justify the prediction on the basis of what has happened so far in the story.	Accept any sensible prediction that links back to the text, for example: The girls go out to see Mr Shenks.	1	A guess not connected with the text	Re-read the text. What has happened so far? What do you think could happen next?
4	Literal Comprehension: Literal Comprehension White A/B	Participate in discussions about books they have listened to or read, recalling the story and making reference to significant events and characters.	Because it has a tag shaped like a bone	1	Another reason not connected to the text	Re-read the story text on page 2. What clue is there that shows us that the object could be a dog collar?
5	Inference: Making Inferences White A/B	Discuss why some events in a story are important and make simple links between items of information.	Because she wasn't actually looking for the dog	1	Any incorrect answer	Think about what Kim was doing and thinking about before her dad came along. Why might she be surprised by what he says?
6	Responding to the Text: Personal Response and Evaluation of Text White A/B	With support, use empathy to help them understand characters and their motivation.	Accept any sensible reason supported by the text, for example: They were worried about him. He was lost. They had been looking for him for ages.	1	A guess that doesn't fit with the text	Re-read the story. Dad and Mr Shenks had been looking for Lancelot for a while. How do you think they felt about it?
7	Language for Effect: Literary Language White A/B	Recognise interesting vocabulary in a text they have listened to or read.	Grinning; beaming (Award 1 mark for each word.)	2	Picking words that don't mean the same as 'smiling' / Only finding one word	Re-read the text and look out for two words that could be replaced by the word 'smiling'.

	Skill	Objective	Accept		Do not award	Question
8	Literal Comprehension: Literal Comprehension White A/B	Participate in discussions about books they have listened to or read, recalling the story and making reference to significant events and characters.	Accept any sensible answer supported by the text, for example: Mr Shenks is old and can't walk the dog so easily now; the dog needs to be walked; the dog likes the girls.	1	An answer that doesn't reflect the text	Re-read the end of the story. What does Mr Shenks say that could be a reason why he asks the girls to walk Lancelot?
9	Language for Effect: Vocabulary Development White A/B	Discuss and clarify the meanings of words, linking new meanings to known vocabulary.	They both spoke at the same time. (Or similar appropriate answer)	1	An answer that shows the child doesn't understand what 'chimed' means in this metaphorical context	Mel and Kim both said the words in speech marks. What other word could we use instead of 'chimed' in this sentence?
10	Themes and Conventions: Text Structure White A/B	With support, can sometimes comment on the appropriateness of the author's choice of title for a poem or story.	Accept any reasoned response that makes sense in the context, for example: It's a good title because Mr Shenks and Lancelot both feature in the story. It's a bad title because the story is mostly about Mel and Kim.	1	No reason given; Reason that doesn't reflect the content of the story	Can you think of at least one reason why it is a good or bad title? Remember that story titles need to fit the story and tell the reader something about it. Does this title do that?
			Total:	12		

White B Marking Guidance: How to Make a Worm Farm

Recommended for: Year 2 Extension

Qu.	Skill Area and Strand	Objective	Answers	Marks	Possible Errors	Advice
1	Literal Comprehension: Literal Comprehension White A/B	Ask and answer questions about books they have listened to or read, often making links between one event or piece of information and another, and where necessary drawing on what they already know or on background information and vocabulary provided by the teacher.	Special composting worms	1	Not retrieving the necessary information from the text to answer correctly	Look in the 'What you need' section for some information about the type of worms you can use in a worm farm.
2	Themes and Conventions: Text Structure White A/B	Able to read a range of non-fiction texts structured in different ways.	To help the reader find the information easily To separate out the things you need clearly (Or similar appropriate answer)	1	Not understanding why bullet points are appropriate here	Think about how bullet points help the reader. Do they make it easier to see what you need?

White B Marking Guidance: How to Make a Worm Farm

© Pearson Education Ltd 2015

3	Inferences: Making Inferences White A/B	Discuss why some events in a text are important and make simple links between items of information. Participate in discussions about books they have listened to or read, making inferences on the basis of what is said and done and listening to what others say.	Because they want to recycle food scraps Because they want to use the compost on their garden (Or similar appropriate answer) (Award 1 mark for each answer.)	2	Only finding one reason Guessing a reason not connected with the text	Read the introduction, before 'What you need'. What are the two ways that worm farms could help us?
4	Literal Comprehension: Sequencing White A/B	Demonstrate understanding of simple cause and effect in fiction and non-fiction texts, discussing sequence of events and explaining how items of information are related.	So that the worms don't get squashed or hurt	1	Any incorrect answer	Which of the answer choices is a reason for putting the worms in last?
5	Inferences: Making Inferences White A/B	Discuss why some events in a text are important and make simple links between items of information.	Because the worm compost stays in the top box and the worms' wee goes down into the bottom box (Or similar appropriate answer)	1	An answer that reveals the child hasn't picked up the reason for having two boxes from the text	Re-read the text. What does it tell us about what ends up in the bottom box and what ends up in the top box?

6	Themes and Conventions: Text Structure White A/B Able to read a range of non-fiction texts structured in different ways.	So it's easy for the reader to see which order to do things in (Or similar appropriate answer)	1	Not understanding why numbered points are appropriate here, to show a sequence of events	Think about what the numbers tell us. How might they help the reader when making the worm farm?
7	Language for Effect: Vocabulary Development White A/B Discuss and clarify the meanings of words, linking new meanings to known vocabulary.	Damp; a little bit wet (Or similar appropriate answer)	1	An answer that shows the child doesn't know what 'moist' means	Re-read the sentence. What might 'moist' mean? Use your dictionary to help you.
8	Literal Comprehension: Literal Comprehension White A/B Ask and answer questions about books they have listened to or read, often making links between one event or piece of information and another, and where necessary drawing on what they already know or on background information and vocabulary provided by the teacher.	**Worms like** Accept any three of the following: fruits, vegetable scraps, eggshells, leaves, tea leaves, and wet, shredded cardboard and paper. **Worms don't like** Accept any three of the following: butter, cheese, meat, fish, fat or bones, citrus peel and onions. (Award 2 marks for all correct, and 1 mark for some correct.)	2	Only some items correct, or a guess unconnected with the text	Look in the section called 'Looking after your worms'. Check what you put in the table against the lists of what worms enjoy eating, and foods to avoid.

9	Literal Comprehension: Information Retrieval White A/B	With support, find specific information on a page of non-fiction text, often using features such as key words, headings, captions etc. appropriately.	Looking after your worms	1	Any other section of the text	Look at the section you chose. Does it have information about when to feed the worms? Where is that information found?
10	Inferences: Making Inferences White A/B	Discuss why some events in a text are important and make simple links between items of information.	Mix it with water and put it on the garden (Or similar appropriate answer)	1	An answer that shows children haven't made the connection between the stated use for worms' wee, and the contents of the bottom box	What ends up in the bottom box? What does the text say you could do with it?
			Total:	12		

Lime A Marking Guidance: The Case of the Horrible Hiccups

Recommended for: Year 2 Extension

Qu.	Skill Area and Strand	Objective	Answer	Marks	Possible Errors	Advice
1	Literal Comprehension: Sequencing Lime A/B	Discussing sequence of events and explaining how items of information are related.	She had woken up late.	1	Any incorrect answer	Re-read the first paragraph and, looking at the first sentence, note what it is that makes Ruby hurry.
2	Language for Effect: Literary Language Lime A/B	Recognise interesting vocabulary.	Accept any four of the following: leapt; ran; threw (on); dashed; grabbed; gobble; crammed (Award 1 mark for two or three correct.)	2	Woke up late	Find and talk about words that actually tell us Ruby is in a hurry, not the words that tell the reader why she is in a hurry.
3	Inference: Making Inferences Lime A/B	Making inferences on the basis of what is said and done.	Accept any answer that indicates that Mum was unhappy / angry / worried / didn't like it	1	Mum wanted her toast back.	Find the word 'warned' and look at what Mum says.
4	Inference: Making Inferences Lime A/B	Making inferences on the basis of what is said and done.	She thought they would go away.	1	She was in a hurry.	Look carefully at what Ruby says to her mum.

No.	Objective	Description	Answer	Mark	Any incorrect answer	Guidance
5	Literal Comprehension: Literal Comprehension Lime A/B	Making links between one event or piece of information and another, and where necessary drawing on what they already know or on background information.	Accept answers that indicate: Ruby is hiccupping; Ruby's hiccups happened in the middle of her sentences; how loud Ruby's hiccups were; the sound Ruby's hiccups made	1	Any incorrect answer	What do you think 'HIC' means?
6	Literal Comprehension: Literal Comprehension Lime A/B	Making links between one event or piece of information and another.	The library	1	She asked Luke / a computer / the computers School	A 'where' question means that the answer will be a place not a person or an object. The question is asking for a specific place and not a general one as in 'school'.
7	Literal Comprehension: Sequencing Lime A/B	Discussing sequence of events and explaining how items of information are related.	Drink with your head upside down: Ruby had a coughing fit Hold your breath: Ruby kept hiccupping, so she couldn't do it Blow into a paper bag: Ruby was told off by a teacher	1	A different combination	The first list shows the order in which things happened in the story. Try to scan the text for information and draw one line at a time.

8	Language for Effect: Vocabulary Development Lime A/B	Miserably	1	Thoughtfully	'Thoughtfully' doesn't recognise Ruby's experiences with the ideas from the first website.
	Clarify the meanings of words, linking new meanings to known vocabulary.			Eventually	'Eventually' doesn't make sense in this context.
				Cheerfully	'Cheerfully' doesn't take into account how Ruby felt after all her efforts failed and she was still hiccupping.
9	Responding to the Text: Personal Response and Evaluation of the Text Lime A/B	Luke had read that scaring someone would stop their hiccups, so he tried to scare Ruby.	1	He wanted to trick her.	This answer doesn't explain fully that Luke knew that scaring Ruby might help stop her hiccups.
	Explain and discuss their understanding, sometimes giving a more detailed account of their opinions.				
10	Inference: Making Inferences Lime A/B	a) Luke had looked for ideas / clues / information to solve the problem of the hiccups. (1 mark)	2	It was a joke.	Look back through the whole story for clues that might link to the word 'detective'.
	Making inferences on the basis of what is said and done.				
	Themes and conventions: Text Structure Lime A/B	b) Because the author wanted it to be like a detective story (1 mark)		Any incorrect answer	Look back at the story. What type of story would use words such as 'clues', 'solved' and 'detective'?
	Comment on the appropriateness of the author's choice of title for a story.				
		Total:	12		

Lime B Marking Guidance: The Night of the Bear
Recommended for: Year 2 Extension

Qu.	Skill Area and Strand	Objective	Answer	Marks	Possible Errors	Advice
1	Literal Comprehension: Literal Comprehension Lime A/B	Ask and answer questions, often making links between one event and another.	She lives in Canada. Maddy and Ben are friends. (Award 1 mark if both are correct and no other boxes are ticked.)	1	Maddy and Ben are both eight years old. She lives in a tent.	Read the text carefully: we know Maddy is eight years old, but we don't know about Ben. Read the text carefully and consider what we know from the text. Do not rely only on pictures for your answer.
2	Inference: Making Inferences Lime A/B	Making inferences on the basis of what is said and done.	Accept answers linked to her age such as: She was sensible enough. She would be able to walk for a long time.	1	An answer that doesn't really relate to the text, e.g. Her dad liked spending time with her. Her dad wanted to invite Ben's dad and they thought they would bring the children.	Use information in the text, rather than just general knowledge.
3	Language for Effect: Vocabulary Development Lime A/B	Discuss and clarify the meanings of words, linking new meanings to known vocabulary.	Every year	1	Any incorrect answer	Use a dictionary to find out what 'annual' means.

Q	Objective	Description	Answer	Marks	Marking notes	Guidance
4	Literal Comprehension: Literal Comprehension Lime A/B	Ask and answer questions, often making links between one event and another.	Maddy; her dad; Ben; Ben's dad	1	Listing fewer than four people / Mentioning the bear	Remember to read the question carefully.
5	Literal Comprehension: Sequencing Lime A/B	Discuss sequence of events and explaining how items of information are related.	1. They put up their tents. 2. Dad hung up his backpack. 3. They toasted marshmallows.	1	Getting the sequence wrong	Look at the sentence beginning: *The first night* ... The word 'after' indicates that hanging up the backpack happened after putting up the tents.
6	Inference: Making Inferences Lime A/B	Making inferences on the basis of what is said and done.	He was scared.	1	He thought it was a joke.	How does Ben ask the question? What do you think the word 'fearfully' means?
7	Literal Comprehension: Literal Comprehension Lime A/B	Ask and answer questions, often making links between one event and another.	Dad's breathing: Soft / Leaves: Rustling / Twigs: Crackling	1	Any incorrect answer	Read the text and find the descriptive words. What do they refer to?
8	Language for Effect: Literary Language Lime A/B	Recognise simple recurring literary language in stories and poetry.	It was <u>pitch black</u> in the tent I was sharing with Dad. It was <u>as dark as a deep cave.</u>	2	Some words not underlined / Whole sentence underlined	Read the sentence aloud, word by word, thinking about the information given. / Read the question again. What is it asking you to do?
9	Responding to the Text: Personal Response and Evaluation of Text Lime A/B	Explain and discuss their understanding, sometimes giving a more detailed account of their opinions.	No Answer should be supported by an explanation, e.g. The noise Maddy heard wasn't a bear: it was just Ben's dad snoring.	1	Yes, with a reason that isn't supported by the text	What do you think about the story and the twist at the end? / If a bear had come to get the marshmallows, it would have been mentioned in the story.

10	Literal Comprehension: Literal Comprehension Lime A/B	Ask and answer questions, often making links between one event and another.	True	False	2	Incorrect boxes ticked	Try to scan the text for each piece of information in order to check.
			✓				
				✓			
			✓				
				✓			
				✓			
		(Award 1 mark for two or three correct.)					

		Total:	12

57

Lime B Marking Guidance: The Night of the Bear

© Pearson Education Ltd 2015